FOLLOW THAT FOOD CHAIN

A GALÁPAGOS ISLAND Food Chain

A WHO-EATS-WHAT Adventure

Rebecca Hogue Wojahn   Donald Wojahn

For Eli and Cal. We hope this answers some of your questions.

There are many links in the chain that created this series. Thanks to Ann Kerns, Carol Hinz, Danielle Carnito, Sarah Olmanson, Paul Rodeen, the staff of the L. E. Phillips Memorial Public Library, and finally, Katherine Hogue

Lerner Publications Company
A division of Lerner Publishing Group, Inc.
241 First Avenue North
Minneapolis, MN 55401 U.S.A.

Website address: www.lernerbooks.com

Library of Congress Cataloging-in-Publication Data

Wojahn, Rebecca Hogue.
    A Galápagos Island food chain : a who-eats-what adventure / by Rebecca
  Hogue Wojahn and Donald Wojahn.
      p.   cm. — (Follow that food chain)
    Includes bibliographical references and index.
    ISBN 978-0-8225-7613-6 (lib. bdg. : alk. paper)
    1. Food chains (Ecology)—Galápagos Islands—Juvenile literature.
  I. Wojahn, Donald. II. Title.
  QH198.G3W65 2010
  577.5′219098665—dc22   2008050218

Manufactured in the United States of America
1 2 3 4 5 6 – BP – 15 14 13 12 11 10

FOLLOW THAT FOOD CHAIN

Contents

Introduction
WELCOME TO THE ISLANDS

The enchanted isles of the Galápagos Islands are hidden in the Pacific Ocean 600 miles (966 kilometers) east of Ecuador. Flying over by plane, you'll see that the islands lay like a chain in the ocean. There are thirteen large islands, six small ones, and dozens of tiny ones called islets. All were created by volcanic eruptions beginning nine million years ago deep under the ocean.

If you visit the island by boat, you'll notice up close the black **lava** rocks and the sandy beaches. You'll see the dry land covered with cactuses, shrubs, and scrubby trees. You might even smell the ash from an erupting volcano. Whatever you do, don't forget your sunscreen! The Galápagos chain is just north of the **equator**, so the sun is strong and hot.

You'll also notice the creatures of the island. As you step off the boat, be prepared to step into a whole different world. These animals don't exist anywhere else on Earth. Millions of years ago, when the islands were just steaming chunks of lava stone, nothing lived on them. But as the years passed, the islands developed a layer of soil. Seeds blew in on the wind, landed in the soil, and sprouted.

Migrating birds were blown off course and found a home here. In time, driftwood and dead trees washed up. Hidden on these floating rafts were snakes, lizards, tortoises, rats, and insects. Their feathers and fur held other seeds that fell in the soil and grew. The animals also ate plants and then pooped out the seeds. That helped grow even more plants.

These plants and animals thrived on the islands, but they were all alone. For millions of years, they lived without contact with the rest of the world. They evolved (changed over time) to be better able to live on the islands' **habitats**. They became some of the world's most unique and unusual **species**. Come meet just a few of them in this book.

EQUATOR

Pacific
Ocean

GALÁPAGOS ISLANDS

N

Charles Darwin

In 1835 Charles Darwin, a British scientist, visited the Galápagos Islands. Darwin came to the islands to study plants and animals. He saw many unusual things—giant tortoises, finches with different types of beaks, and sunflowers growing as tall as trees. Those unusual animals and plants got him thinking. They helped Darwin form his ideas about evolution—how species change over time to fit new environments. After visiting the islands, he wrote a book called *The Origin of Species*. It introduced Darwin's theory of evolution to the rest of the world for the first time.

Choose a
TERTIARY CONSUMER

All the living things on the islands are necessary for their health and survival. From the flies on the black lava rock under your shoes to the Galápagos hawk circling overhead, the living things are all connected. This is called a **food chain** or a **food web**.

In food chains, the strongest **predators** are called **tertiary consumers**. They hunt other animals for food and have few natural enemies. Some of the animals they eat are called **secondary consumers**. Secondary consumers are also predators. They hunt plant-eating animals. Plant eaters are **primary consumers**.

Plants are **producers**. Using energy from the sun, they produce their own food. Plants take in **nutrients** from the soil. They also provide nutrients to the animals that eat them.

Decomposers are insects or bacteria (tiny living things) that break down dead plants and animals. Decomposers change them into the nutrients found in the soil.

The plants and animals in a food chain depend on one another. Sometimes there's a break in the chain, such as when one type of animal dies out. This loss ripples through the rest of the habitat.

Most food web journeys begin at the top of the food chain with a **carnivore**, or meat eater. They are the tertiary consumers. In many food chains, the strongest predators are large **mammals**, such as tigers, wolves, or bears. But most large mammals couldn't survive an ocean crossing to the Galápagos Islands without food or water. On these islands, there aren't any big carnivores like you see in the rest of the world. The tertiary consumers here are few in number. And they come from the ocean and the air.

In this book, when it's time for the tertiary consumer to eat, you pick its meal and flip to the corresponding page. As you progress through the book, don't be surprised if you backtrack and end up where you never expected to be. That's how food webs work—they're complicated. And watch out for those dead ends! When you hit one of those, you have to go back to page 7 and start over with another tertiary consumer.

The main role a plant or animal plays in a Galápagos Island food web is identified by a color-coded shape. Here is the key to that code:

TERTIARY CONSUMER

PRODUCER

SECONDARY CONSUMER

PRIMARY CONSUMER

DECOMPOSER

To choose . . .

. . . a Galápagos hawk, TURN TO PAGE 10.
. . . a Galápagos barn owl, TURN TO PAGE 24.
. . . a great frigate bird, TURN TO PAGE 34.
. . . a Galápagos sea lion, TURN TO PAGE 44.

To learn more about a Galápagos Island food web, GO TO PAGE 47.

SANTA FE RICE RAT *(Oryzomys galapagoensis bauri)*

The Santa Fe rice rat creeps through the dry, scrubby grass. It's finally getting dark. The darker the night gets, the bolder he becomes. He stops to nibble on some seeds. Then he sees something he can't resist. He scurries up to a campers' tent. With some quick gnawing, he is through the lightweight fabric and inside. There's no food here, but there's lots to explore. Like many of the animals of the Galápagos, rice rats are more curious about humans than afraid of them.

Not that long ago, seven **native** species of rats lived on the islands. Then ships carrying the common black rat arrived in the islands. Many of these black rats escaped to shore. No one's sure why, but Galápagos rice rats just don't survive when black rats are around. Maybe black rats infect rice rats with deadly diseases. Or maybe black rats leave no room or food for rice rats. Whatever the reason, only two types of rice rats are left on the islands.

People are trying hard to control the spread of black rats on the island. They want to protect the last two kinds of rice rats.

Last night for dinner, the Santa Fe rice rat chewed on . . .

. . . opuntia cactus pads.
To see what opuntia cactuses are like, TURN TO PAGE 56.

. . . a carpenter bee, cold and slow in the night. To see what another carpenter bee is up to, TURN TO PAGE 13.

. . . seeds from some sunflowers. To see what the sunflowers of the Galápagos Islands are like, TURN TO PAGE 51.

. . . a white-lined sphinx moth tucked in some leaves. To see what another white-lined sphinx moth is up to, TURN TO PAGE 33.

GALÁPAGOS HAWK *(Buteo galapagoensis)*

The Galápagos hawk soars over the island. In the air currents, she barely needs to flap her dark brown wings. She tilts them and glides closer to the ground. She comes to rest on a shrubby tree. But after only a few minutes, a mockingbird starts squawking. The hawk is too close to the mockingbird's nest for comfort. In a few more minutes, the mockingbird's friends and relatives join in. Soon a dozen mockingbirds are complaining loudly about the hawk. They swoop close to her, but not close enough for her to catch one. Eventually, their noise and bluster are too much for the hawk. She flies off.

Her next flight takes her low over a field. She spies three other Galápagos hawks devouring something on the ground next to two humans. She wings in to investigate. Since she is the largest predator on the islands, she has no enemies and isn't afraid of anything. She settles about 5 feet (1.5 meters) from a human hunter.

The hunters aren't after the hawks. They are hunting **feral** goats. These are pet goats that have gone wild and now are damaging the plants of the islands. The Galápagos hawk muscles her way in to feed on the killed feral goat. No hunting today for her. Today's meal was easy.

Last night for dinner, the Galápagos hawk snatched up . . .

. . . bits of a dead Galápagos sea lion on the beach. To see what another Galápagos sea lion is up to, **TURN TO PAGE 44.**

. . . a Santa Fe rice rat investigating a fallen cactus. To see what another Santa Fe rice rat is up to, **TURN TO PAGE 8.**

. . . a great frigate bird swimming through the shallows. To see what another great frigate bird is up to, **TURN TO PAGE 34.**

. . . a young Galápagos tortoise that just dug himself out of his nest. To see what another Galápagos tortoise is up to, **TURN TO PAGE 30.**

. . . a flightless cormorant drying out her wings. To see what another flightless cormorant is up to, **TURN TO PAGE 43.**

. . . a young marine iguana trying to warm up after a cold night. To see what another marine iguana is up to, **TURN TO PAGE 37.**

. . . a Galápagos petrel that had fallen out of his nest. To see what another Galápagos petrel is up to, **TURN TO PAGE 21.**

. . . a Galápagos penguin sunning in the early morning. To see what another Galápagos penguin is up to, **TURN TO PAGE 54.**

CARPENTER BEE
(Xylocopa darwini)

The female carpenter bee meanders through the flowers on a hillside. She is the only kind of bee that lives on the islands. She takes care to visit each blossom. She flies into the center, sucks up some of the flower's sweet nectar, picks up a little pollen on her legs, and then buzzes onto the next bloom.

Her entire day is spent doing this. It may not look like much, but the islands' plant life depends on her visits. By mixing pollen from flower to flower, she helps new flowers and seeds grow. Without plants, the islands' animals would not survive.

As the day grows darker, many of the flowers close their blossoms. The bee takes the hint and heads home. Many bees live together in hives. But the carpenter bee lives alone. Home is a nest dug out of some soft wood in a log. She'll stay snug in there until the sun comes out and the flowers open again in the morning.

Last night for dinner, the carpenter bee sipped on . . .

13

. . . **nectar from opuntia cactus flowers.** To see what opuntia cactuses are like, TURN TO PAGE 56.

. . . **pollen from sunflowers.** To see what the sunflowers of the Galápagos Islands are like, TURN TO PAGE 51.

DECOMPOSERS

Decomposers help to break down the bodies of dead plants and animals. Without them, stacks of dead plants and animals would be everywhere. When a sea lion dies, first scavengers, such as the Galápagos hawk, pick off the remains. Then the flies and insect larva start to work on the tiny bits. Bacteria and fungus help the flesh to rot and break down even further. Eventually, all that's left are bones. The **nutrients** are soaked up in the soil or washed out to sea, where the plants use them to grow.

Last night for dinner, the decomposers feasted on the nutrients from a . . .

Decomposers are breaking down the remains of this sea lion.

. . . a sea lion that died of old age at twenty. To see what another Galápagos sea lion is up to, TURN TO PAGE 44.

. . . a Galápagos hawk that was shot accidentally by a human. To see what another Galápagos hawk is up to, TURN TO PAGE 10.

. . . a blue-footed booby that starved after breaking a wing. To see what another blue-footed booby is up to, TURN TO PAGE 48.

. . . a Galápagos petrel that was attacked by a feral cat. To see what another Galápagos petrel is up to, TURN TO PAGE 21.

. . . a lava lizard egg that didn't hatch. To see what another lava lizard is up to, TURN TO PAGE 16.

LAVA LIZARD *(Tropidurus)*

The lava lizard perches on the head of a Galápagos sea lion. It's the perfect place to be this morning. The sun is bright and warm. Plenty of delicious flies are buzzing around. Slurp—she snags one as it lands on the sea lion's head. And best of all, no pesky predators are going to approach if you're sitting on the biggest animal on the island!

A female lava lizard perches on a rock.

The Eyes Have It

Lava lizards depend on their eyes. They especially notice things that are red and yellow. Scientists think that this is because male lava lizards have yellow on their throats and females have red. Being extra sensitive to these colors helps the lava lizards recognize potential mates.

Lava lizards also notice the slightest movement with their eyes. This comes in handy for watching for predators, as well as for catching speedy insects.

Only—wait! The sea lion rolls up on its front flippers and begins a waddle to the ocean. It's time for the lizard to either strike out on her own or get very wet.

The lizard scuttles down the sea lion's back onto the black lava rock. Except for the patch of red on her throat, the lizard's color almost exactly matches the rough lava rock. Around the island, other lava lizards' colors vary. Their colors match the color of the lava where they live.

The lizard heads into the tall grass at the edge of the lava rock. It's a mistake. Hidden in the grass is a **feral** cat. Almost instantly, the cat pounces. It grabs the lizard's tail. The lizard wriggles free, but she has to leave her tail. The wiggling tail distracts the cat just long enough for the lizard to find safety in a rock crevice. Luckily, her tail will grow back.

The lizard waits for the cat to leave. Once it's gone, she can start looking for her next meal. *Last night for dinner, she munched on . . .*

A male lava lizard watches for a mate.

. . . a white-lined sphinx moth that got damp in the night and couldn't fly. To see what another white-lined sphinx moth is up to, TURN TO PAGE 33.

. . . an ocean skater blown to shore on some driftwood. To see what another ocean skater is up to, TURN TO PAGE 19.

. . . a carpenter bee buzzing around the sea lion's head. To see what another carpenter bee is up to, TURN TO PAGE 13.

OCEAN SKATER
(Halobates robustus)

The ocean skater skims along the edge of the water. His group, or flotilla, is hanging out near the waterlogged roots of a mangrove tree. Some ocean skaters float together in pairs. Others, mostly males, glide over the surface of the water.

The tide is coming in. The water is rising on the roots and leaves. Despite the moving water, the flotilla stays in the same spot, flicking around the roots.

This is a good time for hunting for our ocean skater. Bits of seaweed, driftwood, and dead insects are washing ashore. The incoming water means a skater will be less likely to be dragged out to sea too. The ocean skater pushes off with his hind legs—kind of like he is rowing. In a blink of an eye, he shoots away from the group. He can't fly, but he is able to move quickly across the water—about 5 feet (1.5 meters) in one second. This speed helps him keep out of the reach of predators.

He crunches on bits of a dead bug. He doesn't need much. Although his legs are long, his body's just 0.25 inches (0.6 centimeters) long.

After his meal, he zings back to the flotilla. There's definitely safety in numbers if you're a bug.

Last night for dinner, the ocean skater snacked on . . .

...tiny bits of algae. To learn more about the algae of the Galápagos Islands, TURN TO PAGE 22.

...the leg of a carpenter bee. To see what another carpenter bee is up to, TURN TO PAGE 13.

...the wing of a white-lined sphinx moth. To see what another white-lined sphinx moth is up to, TURN TO PAGE 33.

Surface Tension

So how do ocean skaters stay on the surface of water? Why don't they sink? They are kept afloat by something called surface tension. First of all, their legs are waterproof. They are coated in a substance that pushes the water away. Then, their legs have small hairs covering them that help spread out the insect's weight over a greater area of the water. It's a little like finding yourself on a patch of thin ice. If you try to walk across the thin ice, you'd break through. But if you lie down flat on the ice, you are less likely to end up wet and cold.

GALÁPAGOS PETREL *(Pterodroma phaeopygia)*

Far out over the ocean, a Galápagos petrel tips her wings and banks toward shore. She spent the day gulping down fish and squid in her ocean feeding grounds. But now that it's dusk, she's heading home.

Her home is in the damp ground on the high parts of the island. There she has dug a burrow. Just a few weeks ago, she laid a single egg in it, but it's gone now. It was stolen and eaten by a black rat. That's one of the reasons this is a **DEAD END**. Because of **invasive** species such as cats, dogs, pigs, and black rats, the Galápagos petrel is in danger of becoming **extinct**.

21

New Name but Still Endangered

The Galápagos petrel used to be called the dark-rumped petrel. Scientists once thought it was the same type of petrel that could be found on the Hawaiian Islands. But since then, scientists have decided that the birds are not the same at all. They renamed the two types the Galápagos petrel and the Hawaiian petrel. Whatever scientists call them, they are both still very endangered in the wild.

ALGAE

Algae surround the Galápagos Islands—from microscopic kinds floating in shallow pools to a huge type of seaweed known as kelp. The islands and their animals couldn't survive without algae. They are a source of food for many animals, but algae also help provide oxygen for all of us.

You see, like plants, algae give off oxygen through the process of **photosynthesis**. In photosynthesis, algae draw in a gas called carbon dioxide. Humans and animals give off carbon dioxide when they exhale (breathe out). Carbon dioxide can also be created as dead plants and animals decompose, or break down.

Algae use carbon dioxide to create their food. During this process, they give off oxygen—the gas we need to breathe. Scientists estimate that the oceans' algae provide humans and animals with 70 to 80 percent of all their oxygen!

All algae can be divided into three different kinds: red, green, or brown. Brown algae are the most common algae in the ocean. But they tend to grow in waters more north of the islands. Red algae appear in the deep waters around the Galápagos Islands. Red algae like cool water and little light. And green algae are the least common ocean algae. They are found mostly in bodies of freshwater. The creatures of the islands nibble on green varieties, such as sea lettuce, in the reefs offshore.

Last night for dinner, the algae took in . . .

Red algae makes this island lake look red.

Many Names, Many Uses

Did you know that algae are useful for many other things besides producing oxygen? Throughout history, people have used seaweed (a type of algae) as fertilizers to grow crops, as fuel, and as food. And if you look at a container of ice cream, chances are you'll see an extract from algae listed as an ingredient. Carrageenan is used in milk products to help keep the food creamy. It can also be found in your toothpaste, lotions, makeup, and pet foods.

. . . carbon dioxide exhaled by a Galápagos sea lion. To see what another Galápagos sea lion is up to, TURN TO PAGE 44.

. . . nutrients from a flightless cormorant that was washed out to sea. To see what another flightless cormorant is up to, TURN TO PAGE 43.

. . . nutrients from a dead great frigate bird. To see what another great frigate bird is up to, TURN TO PAGE 34.

. . . nutrients from a Galápagos penguin that was caught in a fishing line and died. To see what another Galápagos penguin is up to, TURN TO PAGE 54.

. . . nutrients that decomposers broke down from dead plants. To learn more about the decomposers of the Galápagos Islands, TURN TO PAGE 14.

To learn more about photosynthesis, TURN TO PAGE 51.

GALÁPAGOS BARN OWL *(Tyto alba punctatissima)*

The Galápagos barn owl glides over dark ground without a sound. Unlike most birds, the edges of her wings' feathers are soft and downy. This muffles any flapping sounds. It also helps her to sneak up on her **prey**.

Tonight it's pitch black out. No moon, no stars. But she's still hunting. When there's no light at all, her eyes can't help her. But her ears can. And they are even more powerful than her eyes.

She drifts lower. Over there—the squeak of a rice rat. The barn owl pounces. She flies away with the rat clamped in her talons. How did she catch it without seeing it? Her ears are in different places on the sides of her head—one high, one low. Each ear also hears different sounds. These differences allow her to pinpoint sounds much better than we—or most other animals—can.

She'll take this rat back to her roost. She lives in a collapsed lava tube—a long cave formed by flowing lava—among the rocks. There she'll swallow her prey whole. All the soft parts of the rat will be digested inside her. She'll cough back up the skull and bones in a pellet. The rocks under her roost are littered with these hard balls of fur and bones.

Last night for dinner, the Galápagos barn owl caught and swallowed . . .

A One-Pound Barn Owl

The Galápagos barn owl is the smallest of the world's barn owls. An adult female is just 13 inches (33 centimeters) tall and weighs less than 1 pound (454 grams). Unlike most birds, the females are bigger than the males. They also have more spots on their front. Both males and females have heart-shaped faces without the ear tufts that most owls have.

25

. . . more Santa Fe rice rats. To see what another Santa Fe rice rat is up to, TURN TO PAGE 8.

. . . a lava lizard that crawled into the wrong niche in the lava rocks. To see what another lava lizard is up to, TURN TO PAGE 16.

. . . a Darwin's finch making his nest too close to dusk. To see what another Darwin's finch is up to, TURN TO PAGE 40.

. . . a Galápagos petrel, ambushed in the rocks. To see what another Galápagos petrel is up to, TURN TO PAGE 21.

. . . a hatchling marine iguana that didn't snuggle up to the rest of the family. To see what another marine iguana is up to, TURN TO PAGE 37.

. . . a young flightless cormorant stretching on the shore. To see what another flightless cormorant is up to, TURN TO PAGE 43.

. . . a blue-footed booby chick pushed out of his nest. To see what another blue-footed booby is up to, TURN TO PAGE 48.

. . . a Galápagos penguin chick roosting on the rocks. To see what another Galápagos penguin is up to, TURN TO PAGE 54.

FISH

The waters around the Galápagos Islands hold an exciting mix of life-forms. The heat of the sun makes the surface of the water warm. But underneath the surface, icy cold currents pull the water along like rivers. The currents also bring extra nutrients to the area. This combination of water temperatures, current, and extra food creates a welcome home for more than 450 kinds of fish. Of these, many, such as the four-eyed blenny, can be found only off the shores of these islands.

Above: A streamer hogfish feeds on a coral reef. *Below:* Various types of fish swim around a reef.

Above: Bronze whaler sharks attack a group of fish. **Below:** A tiger snake eel feeds on a crab as it burrows into the ocean floor.

As you dive underwater, you'll see smaller reef fish, such as angelfish, dart and hide in the cracks in the lava rocks. In the deeper waters, other small fish, such as the surgeonfish, stay safe by swimming in huge groups called schools. The schools shift and move as one in silvery flashes. Bigger fish (such as tuna, barracudas, sharks, and rays), eels, and sea turtles also cruise the waters off the shores of the islands.

Last night for dinner, the fish fed on . . .

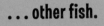

. . . other fish.

. . . **a young Sally Lightfoot crab drifting on the water.** To see what another Sally Lightfoot crab is up to, TURN TO PAGE 58.

. . . **an ocean skater skimming the shallows.** To see what another ocean skater is up to, TURN TO PAGE 19.

. . . **algae floating on the surface.** To learn more about the algae of the Galápagos Islands, TURN TO PAGE 22.

. . . **a white-lined sphinx moth that followed a boat's light out to sea.** To see what another white-lined sphinx moth is up to, TURN TO PAGE 33.

GALÁPAGOS TORTOISE *(Geochelone elephantopus)*

The Galápagos tortoise wakes a few hours after dawn. She crawls out of her dugout space beneath some shrubs. This pit she sleeps in fits her shell, or carapace, perfectly. It's a huge hole. You could fit in it easily. She's almost 400 pounds (181 kilograms) and 4 feet (1.2 meters) long.

She uses her stout, elephant-like legs to push herself onto the "tortoise highway." This is a well-worn path she and other tortoises use to get to the tastiest opuntia cactus field. The highway is busy today. Other tortoises trudge along the path. Nearby, two males hold a face-off. They butt heads. Their carapaces creak like old leather as they rub together. Each one stretches his neck as high as he can. The female Galápagos tortoise walks on.

Two males face off.

Finally, she's at the cactuses. Her long neck allows her to reach the higher pads and flowers. But not all Galápagos tortoises are shaped like her. In fact, there are ten different types of Galápagos tortoises, each a little different size or shape to fit the island habitat it lives in. (The islands once had fourteen types, but some are now **extinct**.)

Just as she settles in to munch, a finch lands on the sand near her. The tiny bird hops over and stands in front of her. It clearly wants something from the tortoise.

Finally, the tortoise responds. She stretches out her legs and neck. The finch hops aboard and pecks at the tortoise. She gulps down the pesky ticks (bloodsucking insects) that cling to the tortoise. When the tortoise is clean and the finch full, the bird flies off.

The tortoise finishes eating. She trundles off down a new path, this time in search of water. It rained last night, so today is a good time for a refill. As she reaches a muddy puddle, she plunges right in. She slurps down the water by the gallons. It'll be enough for her to go months or even a year without drinking again.

Tortoises can go a very long time without eating or drinking. Years ago, that made them ideal meat on ships. Sailors would often stop by the islands, toss a few live tortoises on board, and then use them for fresh meat several months later.

After she's done drinking, our tortoise stays in the puddle. This is the perfect place to stay cool through the heat of the day.

Last night for dinner, the Galápagos tortoise chewed on . . .

. . . **leaves from sunflowers.** To read what the sunflowers of the Galápagos Islands are like, TURN TO PAGE 51.

. . . **more opuntia cactuses.** To read what opuntia cactuses are like, TURN TO PAGE 56.

Lonesome George

One type of Galápagos tortoise is especially rare. The type's scientific name is *Geochelone abingdoni*, and it is native to the island of Pinta. There is just one *Geochelone abingdoni* left. His name is Lonesome George *(right)*. When he dies, his type of tortoise will be extinct.

Or maybe not. Scientists are hoping that they may find a mate for Lonesome George on a different island. In the past, people took tortoises for zoos around the world. Many of them have since been returned to the islands. Scientists are hoping that maybe a *Geochelone abingdoni* was returned to the wrong island and has been living there.

WHITE-LINED SPHINX MOTH *(Hyles lineata)*

The white-lined sphinx moth clings to the leaf. He pumps his new wings in the cool night air. This is the first time he's extended the wings to their full width of 3 inches (7.5 centimeters).

He's lived his whole life near this vine on the humid part of the islands. His egg was laid on one of the vine's leaves. When he hatched as a caterpillar, the leaves were his food. When he got big enough, he crawled down the vine, dug a hole, and built a cocoon around himself. Now he has hatched again and scratched his way back up the plant. As soon as his new wings dry, he'll flit off to start the next phase of his life.

He gives the wings a test shake. Dry! And he's off. He flaps his wings so fast that they make a humming sound. In fact, many people mistake sphinx moths for hummingbirds or bats.

He heads out and away from his vine. Adult sphinx moths live in the dry parts of the islands. Once he reaches his new home, he'll start looking for food. He'll use his long tongue to sip nectar (a sweet liquid) from the flowers.

Tonight for dinner, the white-lined sphinx moth sips . . .

33

. . . nectar from opuntia cactus flowers. To see what opuntia cactuses are like, **TURN TO PAGE 56.**

. . . nectar from the blooms on a sunflower tree. To see what the sunflowers on the Galápagos Islands are like, **TURN TO PAGE 51.**

GREAT FRIGATE BIRD (Fregata minor)

The great frigate bird swoops through the air over the beach. His huge black wings stretch 8 feet (2.5 meters) wide—almost as wide as a small bedroom. The frigate bird narrows his forked tail and spirals in the air. He zooms up right behind a lava gull. He reaches out his black hooked beak and tweaks the gull's tail feathers. The gull squawks. Out of the gull's mouth falls a wad of half-digested fish she was flying home for her chick. The frigate bird dives—and catches the wad neatly in his mouth before it hits the sand. He quickly gobbles it down. After this stolen bit of dinner, the frigate bird settles in a saltbush. Other male frigate birds roost nearby. They're all hoping to find a mate. The frigate bird plumps his feathers. He rears his head back and inflates the red pouch under his neck. It's the size of half a kickball. A female approaches. She is smaller, with red rings around her eyes and white on her chest.

A male frigate bird with his pouch inflated soars through the sky.

34

She flies near him, landing on a branch. He flaps around her. But after a moment, she takes off. She's not interested.

The great frigate bird isn't discouraged. He just puffs himself up more. When the next female stops by, she stays longer. He hooks his wing around her. She stays. She's picked him.

They could gather twigs to make a nest. But why find your own twigs when another bird has already done the work? They wing over to a Galápagos hawk's nest and pull out what they need. When they spy the hawk approaching in the distance, they take off.

Soon, the female will lay one egg on their nest. But their nest is pretty sloppy. Sticks poke out everywhere, and there are huge gaps. Hopefully, it'll be sturdy enough to hold the egg and the chick when it hatches. Frigate bird eggs often slip out of their nests. If that

Birds with Bad Reputations

It's true. Frigate birds often steal food from other animals, especially birds. But they also hunt their own food out of the ocean. Unlike other birds that can dive into the water for their meal, frigates try to get only their beaks wet. That's because their feathers lack the protective waterproof oil that most waterbirds have. One unpredictable wave and a frigate can be drenched. And that could mean his wings are too wet to fly away. He'd be trapped out on the ocean.

A mother frigate bird guards her chick.

happens, the two birds will each go their own way and look for a new mate.

If the egg hatches, the parents guard it for a week. Then they start to leave the nest to hunt (or steal) food. But the poor baby doesn't get to join them. She'll be stuck in the nest, waiting for her parents to return with a meal. After five months, she'll be big enough to fly out with them and start learning their air pirate skills.

Last night for dinner, the great frigate bird swallowed . . .

. . . fish snagged from the top of a wave. To see what the fish near the Galápagos Islands are like, **TURN TO PAGE 27.**

. . . a newborn marine iguana, just crawling out of his burrow. To see what another marine iguana is up to, **TURN TO PAGE 37.**

. . . a newborn Galápagos tortoise on his way to the sea for the first time. To see what another Galápagos tortoise is up to, **TURN TO PAGE 30.**

. . . a blue-footed booby chick that has been left unattended in her nest. To see what another blue-footed booby is up to, **TURN TO PAGE 48.**

. . . a young lava lizard scooting across the sand. To see what another lava lizard is up to, **TURN TO PAGE 16.**

MARINE IGUANA *(Amblyrhynchus cristatus)*

As the sun rises in the sky, the air heats up. The black rocks near the shoreline grow extra hot in the scorching sun. The marine iguana (and a few hundred others) sprawls on the lava stone, soaking up the warm rays of the sun. He is **cold-blooded**, so his body temperature is the same as the air. After a cool night, he must warm himself in the sun.

However, as the day goes by, it becomes *too* hot. The marine iguana raises his body off the rock so the cool breeze can swirl under him. He opens his mouth a little and pants. Still, he's in danger of overheating. He crawls toward the ocean and launches himself into the cold waves. Others join him with their own splashes.

Marine iguanas are the world's only swimming iguanas. Scientists think the iguanas learned to swim when they first arrived on the islands. There probably wasn't much to eat on land, so the iguanas ventured into the water looking for food. The ones that learned to swim survived and passed that ability on to their young. Now marine iguanas prefer the sea.

This marine iguana neatly tucks his legs back and lets his tail do the work. Waving back and forth like a snake, his long tail propels him through the crashing waves. Below him is a reef. He ducks his

head and dives under. Underwater, the reef hides his dinner—algae. Algae are tiny plant-like organisms that live in the water. The marine iguana uses his extra-short snout to trim bits of the algae off the reef stones. He can hold his breath for an hour, but the water's so cold he doesn't risk staying under for longer than ten minutes. Already, he can feel his legs growing weak from the cold.

The marine iguana swims to the surface. Next to him the other iguana feed. One has stayed under too long. That iguana floats on the surface of the water but is too weak to swim. The cold water will continue to lower his body temperature until he dies. He slowly floats out to sea.

Our marine iguana swims back toward shore. He has to move through the booming waves, the looming rocks, and the pesky sea lions who want to tease him. Finally, exhausted, he drags himself to shore. Now, the heat of the sun is welcome again. He presses himself flat on the stone.

As he does, he sneezes. It's not really a sneeze, but it looks and sounds like one. Marine iguanas drink the salty water from the sea. But their bodies have to get rid of the extra salt. They blow the extra salt out of a special gland above their eyes. The salty spray from our iguana's "sneeze" coats his black back. The salt will dry as a white crust.

For now, the marine iguana will rest. He'll soak up the sun so that he can survive the cool night air. Tomorrow, it'll be more of the same.

Last night for dinner, the marine iguana nibbled...

Diving Males and Burrowing Females

Only the largest of the male marine iguanas dive into the sea. The females and younger males stick closer to shore. They are not strong enough to fight the waves. But they find plenty of algae growing on the rocks near shore.

Females also lay their eggs onshore. They must find the perfect spot of sand in which to bury their eggs. They dig and test out many burrows, looking for one with just the right amount of moisture for the eggs. This searching causes many fights between females as they argue over prime egg-laying space.

. . . **other algae, but just the red and green kind.** Never the brown. To learn more about the algae of the Galápagos Islands, TURN TO PAGE 22.

. . . **tiny Sally Lightfoot crabs hidden in the seaweed.** To see what another Sally Lightfoot crab is up to, TURN TO PAGE 58.

DARWIN'S FINCH (Geospizinae)

Zip! Did you see that? That grayish brown tiny bird that flew by? There she is, plucking up seeds. She's a finch. But wait! There's another. He's a male—you can tell because he's darker.

You notice that there are finches all around you. One pecks at the mites and ticks on a marine iguana. Another can be spotted nipping seabirds and drinking their blood. Others crunch leaves and flowers. And look there—that one has snipped off a cactus spine. She's using it as a tool to fish bugs out of the cactus.

How can the same bird have all these different behaviors? That's what the scientist Charles Darwin wondered when he visited the island in 1835. He started to collect these birds to study them up close. He found out that even though these finches all look similar, there are actually thirteen different kinds on the Galápagos Islands. Each one of them has its own call, its own food and, most interesting to Darwin, a different kind of beak. Some were thick and strong, some narrow and needlelike, and others short or wide.

Darwin guessed that the birds all came from the same ancestors. But the birds ate different foods depending on where on the islands they lived. Then their bodies began to **adapt**. That means they changed slowly over time. The changes helped them be successful at getting the food in their habitat. Birds that needed to crack seeds grew thicker beaks, while birds that pecked for insects had narrower ones.

All the finches care for their babies pretty much the same way. See that cactus finch there? The one collecting all the bits of lichen, grass, bark, and twigs? He's building three different nests all at once. They are all ball-shaped with a hole in the side for a door.

Look! A female went in one of his nests. She's picked him! Now, he'll take care of her and bring her food. When the babies are born, he'll bring them seeds, grubs, and berries too. He'll also help to keep their house

A medium ground finch

Finch Beaks

Darwin's finches live all over the Galápagos Islands. Over a long period of time, the finches' beaks changed. The birds adapted to fit the food available in their habitats. This chart shows some of the different sizes and shapes of beaks.

The cactus finch eats insects and parts of the Opuntia cactus. It uses its long, thin beak to search the cactus flowers for bugs.

The large ground finch eats mostly seeds. Its strong, thick beak can crush hard seed shells.

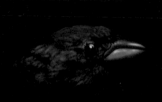

The woodpecker finch uses its beak to grip sticks or cactus spines. It uses the sticks to dig insects from holes in trees and cactuses.

The vegetarian finch eats plants and flowers. Its beak is meant for soft fruit, but it's strong enough for the occasional insect snack.

A sharp-beaked ground finch draws blood from a masked booby.

nice and neat. Just like human babies, those finch babies poop a lot. The parents clean up by carrying all the poop out of the nest each day.

After about two weeks, the babies are big enough that the mom leaves. Sometimes she'll even start a new family with a different dad. But the dad finch will still watch over his nestlings. Eventually, after two more weeks, the babies are grown up enough to be on their own. And then, sometimes, the first male finch even goes to help out with the mom's new family!

Last night for dinner, the finches ate . . .

. . . **sunflower seeds.** To see what the sunflowers of the Galápagos Islands are like, **TURN TO PAGE 51.**

. . . **dead skin plucked from the back of a marine iguana.** To see what another marine iguana is up to, **TURN TO PAGE 37.**

. . . **opuntia cactus flowers.** To see what the opuntia cactuses of the Galápagos Islands are like, **TURN TO PAGE 56.**

. . . **an ocean skater washed up onshore.** To see what another ocean skater is up to, **TURN TO PAGE 19.**

. . . **a white-lined sphinx moth with an injured wing.** To see what another white-lined sphinx moth is up to, **TURN TO PAGE 33.**

. . . **the blood of a great frigate bird, pecked from its back.** To see what another great frigate bird is up to, **TURN TO PAGE 34.**

. . . **a carpenter bee, nabbed while it was gathering pollen.** To see what another carpenter bee is up to, **TURN TO PAGE 13.**

FLIGHTLESS CORMORANT (*Phalacrocorax harrisi*)

The flightless cormorant stands on the shore, stretching his wings wide to dry them. His wings are short compared to his body size. The feathers are thin and ragged. He doesn't need to really dry his wings at all. Anyone can see that they are way too skimpy to ever get the cormorant off the ground. But drying them off is a habit that's left over from his ancestors. The ancestors of the flightless cormorant could once fly and needed dry wings to do so.

Seeing a flightless cormorant on the beach like this is a very rare thing. That's right—they are an **endangered** species. And this is a *DEAD END*.

For thousands of years, flightless cormorants didn't have any land predators on the islands. They stopped flying because they didn't need to escape. Over time, their wings grew weak, and they lost the ability to fly.

But when people started arriving on the islands, they brought dogs and cats. Some of those dogs and cats became **feral**. They hunt the birds of the islands. And because these cormorants can't fly away anymore, they are very easy **prey**.

GALÁPAGOS SEA LION
(Zalophus californianus wollebaeki)

A female *(left)* and male sea lion

The Galápagos sea lion playfully nips the Galápagos penguin as it glides by in the water. The sea lion's not hunting, just bored. The penguin zips away, and the sea lion looks for his next form of entertainment. As he does, he cruises through the waves, just along a patch of beach. When he gets to the invisible boundary of his territory, he barks and flips back. He'll splash his way to the other edge of his territory. Along the way, he bodysurfs a little, just for fun.

Onshore fifteen female sea lions bask in the sun. A sixteenth one is in the shallow water. She is watching several sea lion pups as they explore. They're not all hers. She is babysitting the younger generation of the **colony**.

Our sea lion is the male, or bull, of the colony. This is *his* stretch of beach. He patrols it very seriously. He doesn't even pause to eat. In fact, it's been a while since he's had a meal.

Wait! What's that? A shark fin has popped up. The sea lion barks and rushes at the small shark. Meanwhile, onshore the babysitting sea lion hurries the youngsters out of the water.

The bull sea lion splashes toward the shark. The bull sea lion, at 700 pounds (318 kilograms), is the biggest animal on the islands. And this is a small shark. It quickly gives up and swims off in search of an easier meal.

The shark scare has taken a lot out of the bull sea lion. And he's not going to get a rest any time soon. A second male sea lion lurks just beyond the colony's borders. This second male is without a colony. But he'd like one.

The second male rushes inland. He barks and strikes a pose on the beach. The first male galumphs toward him. They push and bite at each others' thick necks. The second sea lion draws blood. It doesn't take long. The first sea lion is just too exhausted. He retreats to the sea, bleeding from the intruder's bites.

Now he'll head out on his own. The second sea lion will take control of this part of the beach and this colony. Bulls may only rule a colony for a few days, weeks, or months. It's not permanent. While our sea lion is alone, he'll eat a few fish, maybe join a bachelor (all-male) colony, or even start looking for a new colony. Meanwhile, he can always find penguins and iguanas to chase.

Last week for dinner, the sea lion gulped down . . .

Sea Lion Pox

The bull sea lion that got bit will be fine, unless his wounds get infected with a new disease called sea lion pox. Scientists think the disease is transmitted by mosquitoes to open wounds. Once infected, the sea lions get lumps under their skin. They become weak and even paralyzed. In the end, they die of starvation because they can't swim to eat. Scientists aren't sure how this new disease began. But luckily, they see signs that some sea lions are developing the ability to fight off the disease.

45

. . . **fish—almost a whole school of them.** To see what other fish near the island are up to, TURN TO PAGE 27.

. . . **a Galápagos penguin that zipped by underwater a little too closely.** To see what another Galápagos penguin is up to, TURN TO PAGE 54.

. . . **a Sally Lightfoot crab whose shell was still soft.** To see what another Sally Lightfoot crab is up to, TURN TO PAGE 58.

AN ISLAND FOOD WEB

On the Galápagos Islands, energy moves around the food chain from the sun to plants, from plants to plant eaters, and from animals to the creatures that eat them. Energy also moves from dead animals to the plants and animals that draw nutrients from them.

47

BLUE-FOOTED BOOBY (Sula nebouxii)

The blue-footed booby skims the waves. He's part of a flock, all flying together. Without a sound, the group suddenly makes a right turn and climbs higher in the air. Then, all at once, the group tucks their heads and dives straight toward the sea. The booby stretches his wings and feet back and extends his neck. His dart shape is so streamlined that he barely makes a splash as he hits the water at almost 60 miles (97 km) per hour. Good thing he has a special air sac in his head. Otherwise, at those speeds, diving could injure his brain.

The flock finishes their dive underwater. Their beaks neatly grab up fish from a school 6 feet (2 meters) under. Coming up, they break free from the water's surface and continue their flight.

The male booby wings off in a different direction from the flock. Back onshore, a female booby waits for him. But before the male booby reaches their home, a frigate bird flaps out of a tree. It chases him, hoping he might give up the meal he's carrying back to his mate. The booby darts and swerves, but the frigate bird nips at his wings.

Finally, the booby reaches his mate on the beach. The frigate bird takes off in a new direction, looking for something else to chase.

Here on the sandy soil, the female booby is carefully holding their two eggs on her wide blue webbed feet. There's no nest, just a circle of white bird poop around the spot on the ground where they will raise their chicks.

The male says hello to the female by reaching out and touching the tip of his beak to hers. It looks almost like a kiss. She rolls her tummy back to show off what happened while he was away. A scrawny naked chick peeks out! There are two more eggs under her. But since she laid them five days apart, they'll hatch at different times.

This chick is too young and too naked to venture out on her own. She needs her mother's and father's heat to stay alive. Eventually, the white circle of poop will be her and her siblings' boundary. If they cross the line, they'll be in serious trouble. Their parents won't accept them back in the nest. Sometimes, if there's not enough food, a chick will even push another chick over the line. That leaves more food for the remaining chicks to eat.

But right now, there's enough for everyone. The male shares his fish with the female. Then he takes off to find the new chick's first meal.

Last night for dinner, the blue-footed booby tossed down . . .

. . . an ocean skater skimmed from a lagoon. To see what another ocean skater is up to, **TURN TO PAGE 19.**

. . . **more fish.** To see what the fish near the Galápagos Islands are like, **TURN TO PAGE 27.**

. . . **a Sally Lightfoot crab.** To see what another Sally Lightfoot crab is up to, **TURN TO PAGE 58.**

Red Booby, Blue Booby

The blue-footed aren't the only boobies of the Galápagos. The islands are also home to the red-footed and masked boobies. But the blue-footed boobies probably were the first boobies on the islands. They fish from the sea and make their nests directly on the ground. They were able to live on the island even when it was just rock. The red-footed and masked boobies, on the other hand, need trees and bushes to make their nests. That means they probably arrived later, once the islands started to grow plants.

SUNFLOWERS
(Scalesia)

Have you ever munched on sunflower seeds? Those seeds come from the broad, round head of the sunflower plant. Those tall plants from backyard gardens grow on the Galápagos Islands too. The seeds were blown here millions of years ago and landed in the soil.

But like many species, that was only the beginning for the sunflower plants of the islands. The plants, depending on where they grew, developed different sizes and shapes. Now, when you visit the islands, you'll see members of the sunflower family towering

51

sunlight

carbon dioxide

oxygen

water

Plants make food and oxygen through photosynthesis. Plants draw in carbon dioxide (a gas found in air) and water. Then they use the energy from sunlight to turn the carbon dioxide and water into their food.

A sunflower
tree forest

overhead 30 feet (9 meters) high. Others just come up to your chest. Some sunflower plants have more than three hundred small white flowers. Others have fewer but larger blooms. In all, twenty different kinds have developed from one single ancestor.

Last night for dinner, the sunflowers soaked in . . .

. . . **nutrients released into the soil by decomposers.** To learn more about the decomposers of the Galápagos Islands, **TURN TO PAGE 14.**

. . . **nutrients from a Darwin's finch that died from being injured by a feral dog.** To see what another Darwin's finch is up to, **TURN TO PAGE 40.**

. . . **nutrients from a dead Galápagos barn owl.** To see what another Galápagos barn owl is up to, **TURN TO PAGE 24.**

. . . **nutrients from a dead Galápagos hawk.** To see what another Galápagos hawk is up to, **TURN TO PAGE 10.**

. . . **nutrients from a Santa Fe rice rat, killed by a feral cat.** To see what another Santa Fe rice rat is up to, **TURN TO PAGE 8.**

GALÁPAGOS PENGUIN *(Spheniscus mendiculus)*

A penguin in the heat of the Galápagos Islands? Yes, that's right. The Galápagos penguin is the northernmost penguin on Earth. However, they may not be here for long. This is a **DEAD END**. Galápagos penguins are in danger of becoming **extinct**.

The weather is the biggest problem for these penguins. Every so often, the winds that blow across the Pacific Ocean die down. This effect is called **El Niño**. El Niño changes the currents of the water. The cold water the penguins love to swim and feed in disappears. In El Niño years, the water around the islands can be much warmer. The change in temperature kills the **plankton** that fish eat. The fish move to deeper waters. And the fish-eating penguins are left without food.

El Niño is a natural cycle of Earth, but people are changing that cycle. Global warming is causing El Niño to happen more and more often. As a result, penguins have less time to recover in between cycles.

Oil Spill

The world was really worried for the Galápagos penguins back in 2001. That's when an oil tanker hit some rocks near the islands. The rocks tore into the ship, and oil spilled out into the water. If penguins swim through an oil spill, the oil sticks to their feathers. Their feathers are no longer waterproof. It also clogs up the air spaces between the feathers, which is what keeps penguins from getting too cold or too hot. They can't survive in either of these conditions. Luckily, the oil spill didn't drift to where the penguins lived on the islands. But it did get a lot of people thinking hard about how to better protect endangered animals of the islands.

55

OPUNTIA CACTUS *(Opuntia)*

All opuntia cactuses have wide, flat pads with long thorns on them. But that's about all they have in common on the Galápagos Islands. There are six different kinds on the islands, and like many other species, this plant has evolved into many different sizes and shapes. Some grow as tall trees, keeping their pads safe from munching, crunching tortoises and lizards. Others grow wide as shrubs to soak in more sun. One type, *Opuntia saxicola*, is critically **endangered** because of wild goats and cattle churning up the soil.

Like all plants, opuntia cactuses draw nutrients from the soil to help make their food. ***Last night for dinner, the opuntia cactus soaked up . . .***

. . . **nutrients released into the soil by decomposers.** To learn more about the decomposers of the Galápagos Islands, TURN TO PAGE 14.

. . . **nutrients from a Galápagos hawk chick that fell out of its nest and died.** To see what another Galápagos hawk is up to, TURN TO PAGE 10.

. . . **nutrients from a dead Galápagos barn owl.** To see what another Galápagos barn owl is up to, TURN TO PAGE 24.

. . . **nutrients from a Galápagos tortoise that died of old age at 150.** To see what another Galápagos tortoise is up to, TURN TO PAGE 30.

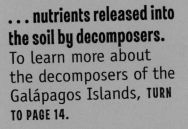

SALLY LIGHTFOOT CRAB (Grapsus grapsus)

Sally Lightfoot crabs speckle the rocks along the shore. The younger ones are black or dark brown. Those colors make it harder for predators to see the crabs on the black lava rocks. The grown-ups are just about every color of the rainbow. There's a red one, with blue and green on the edges of its shell. His neighbor is brown and yellow. Some are spotted, and some are striped. All have either pink or blue eyes and have five pairs of legs.

One tiptoes down to the water. A dead fish floats in a puddle near shore. The crab is only 3 inches (8 centimeters) long, and the fish is almost twice that. But the crab pinches the fish in his front claw and tugs and pulls. Once the fish is out of the water, the crab starts yanking off scraps of meat. He tucks the bits into his mouth. Other crabs join him. There's enough to go around.

Last night for dinner, the Sally Lightfoot crab ate . . .

58

By Sea and by Shore

The very youngest Sally Lightfoot crabs aren't on the rocks. They're still in the ocean. Female crabs swim out into the water to lay thousands of tiny eggs. These eggs hatch as larva—the worm stage before adulthood. The crab larvas float in the water as tiny plankton. Eventually, they'll grow bigger and the ocean's currents will wash them ashore where they'll then spend the rest of their lives.

. . . **fish, big or small, dead or alive.** To read what the fish around the Galápagos Islands are like, TURN TO PAGE 27.

. . . **a drowned white-lined sphinx moth floating in a pool of water.** To see what another white-lined sphinx moth is up to, TURN TO PAGE 33.

. . . **a carpenter bee whose wings got wet and couldn't fly.** To see what another carpenter bee is up to, TURN TO PAGE 13.

. . . **bits from a dead Galápagos penguin.** To see what another Galápagos penguin is up to, TURN TO PAGE 54.

. . . **nibbles off a dead marine iguana.** To see what another marine iguana is up to, TURN TO PAGE 37.

. . . **an ocean skater that didn't skate fast enough.** To see what another ocean skater is up to, TURN TO PAGE 19.

GLOSSARY

adapt: to change along with changes in one's habitat. An animal adapts so that it can better survive in its environment.

carnivore: an animal that eats other animals

cold-blooded: a term for animals that use outside energy, such as heat from the sun, to warm their body temperature

colony: a group of plants or animals of one type that live together

decomposers: living things, such as insects or bacteria, that feed on dead plants and animals

El Niño: a weather pattern that brings extra rain and warm waters to the Galápagos Islands

endangered: close to dying out

equator: an imaginary circle around Earth that is exactly halfway between the North Pole and the South Pole

evolution: a scientific theory about the way species change over long periods of time

extinct: no longer existing

feral: animals once kept by humans that have gotten loose and live in the wild

food chain: a system in which energy is transferred from the sun to plants and to animals as each eats and is eaten

food web: many food chains linked together

habitats: areas where a plant or animal naturally lives and grows

invasive: a species that has moved into an area and threatens the existence of native species

lava: rock that is so hot it is a liquid. Inside Earth, the hot rock is called magma. When it reaches the surface of Earth, it is called lava.

mammals: animals that have hair and feed their babies milk from their bodies

native: a type of plant or animal that occurs naturally in an area

nutrients: substances, especially in food, that help a plant or animal survive

photosynthesis: a process by which a plant uses sunlight, carbon dioxide, and water to make its own food

plankton: a collection of small living things that drift in the ocean

predators: animals that hunt and kill other animals for food

prey: animals that are hunted for food by other animals

primary consumers: animals that eat plants

producers: living things, such as plants, that make their own food

secondary consumers: small animals and insects that eat other animals and insects

species: a group of related animals or plants

tertiary consumers: animals that eat other animals and that have few natural enemies

FURTHER READING AND WEBSITES

Blum, Mark. *Galápagos in 3-D*. New York: Chronicle Books, 2001. The wildlife of the Galápagos above and below the surface of the water jumps out at you in three-dimensional images in this book.

Destination: Galápagos Islands
http://www.pbs.org/safarchive/galapagos.html
Take a virtual field trip to the Galápagos Islands at this website.

Explore Galápagos
http://school.discoveryeducation.com/schooladventures/Galapagos/
Watch a short video of Galápagos creatures, take a quiz, and learn all sorts of interesting facts at this website.

Heller, Ruth. *Galápagos Means "Tortoises."* San Francisco: Sierra Club Books for Children, 2000. The author-illustrator features twelve of the Galápagos Islands's more famous creatures in poems and colorful illustrations.

Jacobs, Francine. *Lonesome George, the Giant Tortoise*. New York: Walker, 2003. Meet Lonesome George, the last Galápagos tortoise of his kind left anywhere in the world.

Junior Zone
http://www.gct.org/children.html
A site just for kids that features animal fact sheets, quizzes, and more.

Kids' Corner
http://www.darwinfoundation.org/en/library/children/kids
Find answers to questions you may have about the Galápagos Islands at this website.

Lawson, Kristan. *Darwin and Evolution for Kids: His Life and Ideas with 21 Activities*. Chicago: Chicago Review Press, 2003. Explore Darwin's theory of evolution through these hands-on activities.

Pascoe, Elaine. *Into Wild Galápagos*. Chicago: Blackbirch Press, 2004. Visit the Galápagos Islands with host Jeff Corwin in this book.

Sis, Peter. *Tree of Life*. New York: Farrar, Straus, and Giroux, 2003. This award-winning illustrated book shares the life, work, and ideas of Charles Darwin.

SELECTED BIBLIOGRAPHY

2008 IUCN Red List of Threatened Species. N.d. http://www.iucnredlist.org (June 26, 2008).

Charles Darwin Foundation. 2006. http://www.darwinfoundation.org/ (June 26, 2008).

De Roy, Tui. *Galápagos: Islands Born of Fire*. Toronto: Warwick, 1998.

Galápagos Conservation Trust. 2008. http://www.gct.org/index.html (June 26, 2008).

Gelman, Rita Golden. *Dawn to Dusk in the Galápagos: Flightless Birds, Swimming Lizards, and Other Fascinating Creatures*. New York: Little, Brown, 1991.

Jackson, Michael H. *Galápagos: A Natural History*. Calgary: University of Calgary Press, 2001.

Myers, Lynne Born, and Christopher A. Myers. *Galápagos: Islands of Change*. New York: Hyperion, 1995.

Steadman, David W., and Steven Zousmer. *Galápagos: Discovery on Darwin's Islands*. Washington, DC: Smithsonian, 1988.

Stewart, Paul D. *Galápagos: The Islands That Changed the World*. DVD. London: BBC Warner, 2007.

Tagliaferro, Linda. *Galápagos Islands: Nature's Delicate Balance at Risk*. Minneapolis: Twenty-First Century Books, 2001.

INDEX

Photo Acknowledgments

The images in this book are used with the permission of: © Alexander van Deursen-Fotolia.com, pp. 1, 4–5, 6–7, 9, 12, 15, 18, 20, 23, 26, 29, 32, 36, 39, 42, 46, 50, 53, 57, 59; © Bill Hauser/Independent Picture Service, pp. 5, 41 (left), 51 (bottom right); © Pete Oxford/naturepl.com, p. 8; © iStockphoto.com/ David Thyberg, p. 10; © age fotostock/SuperStock, pp. 11, 16, 33, 43, 49; © David Hosking/FLPA, p. 13; © Nick Garbutt/NHPA/Photoshot, p. 14; © Tui De Roy/Minden Pictures, pp. 17, 28 (top), 35, 41 (right), 48; Lanna Cheng, Scripps Institution of Oceanography, UC San Diego, p. 19; © Alan Greensmith/ardea.com, p. 21; © Wolfgang Kaehler/CORBIS, p. 22; © INTERFOTO Pressebildagentur/ Alamy, p. 25; © Pete Oxford/Minden Pictures, p. 27 (top); © WorldFoto/Alamy, p. 27 (bottom); © Mark Harding/Peter Arnold, Inc., p. 28 (bottom); © 2009 Norbert Wu/www.norbertwu.com, p. 30; © Brandon Cole/Visuals Unlimited, Inc., p. 31; AP Photo/Charles Darwin Foundation, Heidi Snell, p. 32; © Rosemary Calvert/Photographer's Choice/Getty Images, p. 34; © Pacific Stock/SuperStock, p. 37; © Tom Brakefield/SuperStock, p. 38; © Gerald & Buff Corsi/Visuals Unlimited, Inc., p. 40; © Kevin Schafer/Stone/Getty Images, p. 44; © David Cavagnaro/Peter Arnold, Inc., p. 51 (top); © Michael Lustbader/ Photo Researchers, Inc., p. 51 (bottom left); © S. E. Cornelius/Photo Researchers, Inc., p. 52; © Arthur Morris/Visuals Unlimited/Getty Images, p. 55; © John R. Kreul/Independent Picture Service, p. 56; © iStockphoto.com/ Jeremy Lessem, p. 58. Illustrations for game board and pieces © Bill Hauser/ Independent Picture Service.

Front Cover: © Alexander van Deursen-Fotolia.com (background); © Jim Ballard/ Photographer's Choice/Getty Images (left); © iStockphoto.com/John Bayliss (second from left); © iStockphoto.com/Yaiza Fernandez Garcia (second from right); © Kevin Schafer/Riser/Getty Images (right).

About the Authors

Don Wojahn and Becky Wojahn are school library media specialists by day and writers by night. Their natural habitat is the temperate forests of northwestern Wisconsin, where they share their den with two animal-loving sons and two big black dogs. The Wojahns are the authors of all twelve books in the Follow that Food Chain series.